’sophie

the

coach

house

press

toronto

'sophie

lola

lemire

tostevin

Copyright ©
Lola Lemire Tostevin 1988

Published with
the assistance of
the Canada Council and
the Ontario Arts Council.

Cover image, 'Musik' by
Hans Baldung Grien

Canadian Cataloguing in
Publication Data

Tostevin, Lola Lemire.
'sophie

Poems.
ISBN 0-88910-323-2

I. Title.

PS8589.O6758S66 1988
C811'.54   C88-093426-3
PR9199.3.T68S66 1988

for Jerry

she carries a book
but it is not the tome
of the ancient wisdom
— H.D.

/

listening to Lady Day you forget about lyrics hear
the mystery of voice trace in time a space between
the lines one note above one note below the melody
flowers beyond measure too marvelous for words give
me more and more and then some

on a postcard photograph on my desk gardenias
stick out from the side of her head like antennas
no sound must have gone past her

this morning I placed a bunch of gardenias by my
typewriter looking for the same intoxicating scent
that must have hovered about her scent of jasmine
jazz that mines the slow unfurling of delicate petals
beating time into unknown space

listening to Billie you forget about words sweet
strains don't explain you know what it means

beyond my window a bird is tracing against the sky
the mystery of flight as near as words I move closer
to you

I write because I can't sing I am the book exiled
from my voice in search of a melody but like the woman
who is blind because her eyes are filled with seeing
and like the woman who is deaf because her ears are
filled with hearing I am mute because my voice is filled
with words and unlike music I can only be understood
and not heard

as *These Our Mothers* have said we cannot hide
from ourselves the fictional character of the first A
but neither can I hide the love and the endurance
of that fiction I write the letter *a* as my ancestral
cry cry of the *anima* a vociferous bird from Patagonia
whose beak is a remedy for those whose words fall out
of their mouth too early or too late

I echo the bird's song with eloquence oracular mood
of the loon invent music to the measure of its breath
but because I am word it will never be heard

*

harmony doesn't exist before the lyre
the village wizard said as she placed

seven pebbles

on my tongue and sealed my mouth
with moss from a dead woman's skull

anointed me with weapon salve
to cure the wound through that which caused it

seventh daughter of a seventh daughter
she understood the ancient art of alchemy

that extracts from stones a substance
reducible to its most perfect form

seven letters

that put to the mouth the sounding
and O how that sound surrenders

in spite of being tone deaf
the song was a ruse to please

from the utterances that came
they perceived a sound

that moved them
and they were frightened

'but the Incantatrix speaks
tongues' the Zealots said

so they swam the witch
and the witch sank as proof

of her innocence but then I
would have drowned in water

held in the palm
of your open cupped hand

/

how did my desire come to wear your face flesh
of your flesh bone of your bone how eerily we
resemble your angel spinning on the sharp point
of your needle keeping time to the deathwatch beat

I live your death you die my life I live your death
you die my life ah ecstasy … is what Eros
that little fat kid always flying beyond the realm
of reason would have you believe …

ecstasy (like poetry) casts its line in the form
of an image an illusion to stand outside itself
wishing the very act of naming will prove the very
act of loving to be true thinking you love
therefore I am

/

once the word was invented it was just a matter of
time before we all set out to find the real thing
and like the omnipotent being that brings itself into
existence you walked in stood your post ceased to be
a figment of my imagination

what did you change from? which game? whose power
of enchantment grew out of whose chimera?

your lion's head
the body of a goat
a dragon's tail
your face a fable

your phrases tracing shackles around my thin shin bones

when it's a matter of getting to the point to the
source you outrun me curious courser swift as the
arrow you follow while I crawl at the tortuous pace
of the crooked foot tortoise in search of the sound
your arrow makes when it reaches then wrenches from
the real thing

/

desire is a phantom limb
is voice on the phone
is junction between body and saying what might have been
is memory wanting to repeat itself
thigh nipple cock wanting to enter
their story again

                    the symmetry of their positions

back belly small shallow bowls
that fit so well the contours
of this writing and sets in motion
a woman's hand
                    ear to heart

is penetration that utters
your name until it begins to forget

who is this you framed by my lips?
(who is missing from this picture?)
your absence as looming as your presence was
the mouth emptied as it carries
to their conclusions her thoughts

/

when pleasures of the mind keep dwelling
on pleasures of the body two of us sipping
cold white wine at an outdoor *café* on Spetsai …

except it's twenty years later and I am standing
in a back alley waiting for my old frail dog
on the coldest morning in recorded history feeling
cynicism gradually give way to stoicism which is
just another way of saying the body has undergone
another narrowing fire no longer taken literally
as one of its four elements

when you stand in back alleys you go over conversations
you've never had such as last night when you said
c'mon get real

what do you mean by real?

that this table is solid

and this ice in the heart is it real?

as solid as the table

two of us face to face
in the manner of a table
                              a chair

taking great care not to say the wrong thing each thing
so different when not spoken differently but even the stoic
old terrier must yearn for a time that held less truth
spring when drop by drop the heart unwinds its waterclock

/

mindless the heart
is as useless as an isolated
eye

the woman sitting across from me at the Yamato Tea
Room makes a point of saying she doesn't like intellect
in poetry and my chronic paranoid state doesn't know
whether to be flattered or insulted but my first instinct
is to floor her say something brilliant something to the
effect that the genesis of emotion and intellect are
correlative can only develop through reciprocal adaptation

instead my eye wanders to the perfection of a teapot
on the table the way the eye knows instinctively about
teapots at a distance then the mind in the shape of a hand
follows in the same relation that the eye has to touch

*

Pythagoras believed the soul to be immortal
and as a member of the Pythagorean Society 550 BC
which admitted both men and women on the strength
of their deductive reasoning I am also of this belief

immortality fatal to the hope of release

to this day I abide strictly by the rules:

Not to pick up what has fallen.

Not to stir the fire with iron.

Not to look in a mirror by a light.

Not to touch a white cock.

Not to eat the heart.

*

when a body attracts a body with a force
proportional to the distance that exists
between them the laws that govern their fall
are even more beautiful and intricate
than the stars above
                    pi in the sky

and bodies as obedient as any other
to the laws of gravitation tilt
a few degrees to the west
                        wobble

are lost forever since the earth
slipped a little
as we fell

/

five days of constant rain Newton's
monochromatic rays incessantly drawn

until this afternoon a mote in a sunbeam
where there is no wind and a dozen

long stemmed roses in the wide mouth
of a Mason jar

where at the heart of each flower
there is nothing but heart that opens

without reason tonight the moon
big as an apple about to fall

/

Kh*ien* *chienne* dragon on the wing in the sky returns
everything and everyone to its true nature
                                        bitch

howling at the moon invents her own small vocabulary
maps out her little bits of heaven

at a friend's annual bash I sit while everyone dances
rasp at my throat
smell of dog piss at my feet
too weary to play Maenad to Bacchus
or Helen having just left Paris behind

will they ever come back ever again the long long dances
on through the dark till the dim stars wane? shall I feel
the dew on my throat and the stream of wind in my hair?
shall our white feet meet and gleam in the dim expanses?

/

a woman having a drink late at night wonders
what he's up to and if given the same event
in a different part of the country could the two
not be happening at the same time? she wonders
how common sense has come to think of itself as
a little rum a little *nachtmusik* and small gestures
that persist through space and time

she knows she shouldn't be doing this

she should be writing a poem in which she situates herself
in terms of a desire that passes on through writing
but each time she begins to write she feels she has to reinvent
the world and even old Archimedes given a lever and a fixed
point only had to move it a few inches she wonders

how she came to this place between writing as body
and writing as erasure of the body she wonders
if passivity and passion stem from the same root

she follows the imaginary path of a gesture
that promises to recite their archaic history
the way an extinct animal is reconstructed
from the single facet of a bone

/

she writes to make a name for herself
then loses it in the writing

forges an image that throws her out of herself
to fill the hiatus between extremes of loving

dons a mask of a woman
to prove that's what she is

what does a woman want?
the question asks too little

for Lisa

your silences never lured foreign sailors into Cyrene
it was not in your song that drowned men dwelled when
they set out to plow the seas *femme fish*

when they imagined you destitute of legs and pelvis
wailing in the dark of lagoons it was not you that made
their death please with only bubbles escaping from your beak

for had they found you dear daughter it would have been
on a dry plain somewhere outrunning the okapi maybe
just south of the Sahara

and like the long mute throats of giraffes your slender
fingers would have rubbed and wrapped themselves around
their fingers to compensate for the absence of your song

/

the gardenia by my typewriter is in full bloom has grown
to its ideal form conformed to the patterns within while
Pandora trespasses the spheres thinks up alternatives a yet
to come

in the stillest heat the kitten sits on my desk objects
to the sound of words taking shape on the page doesn't need
them to carry him to an image meows from a place where he's
himself which has nothing to do with anything else place
of pure light where the blind feel the clumsy shapes of things
before they are given names before curiosity killed the cat

eight lives ago the cat was white but now except for one
remaining spot he's black so as far as I know we only have
one life to go

/

the chimes that hang on the deck overlooking the Skootamatta
are the chimes I used to hear in the twelfth century temple
garden that Priest Honen established on the eastern hill
of what was once the Imperial City of Kyoto except then
the pine trees were twisted and gnarled as if holding
a memory of the wind while here they stretch upwards as
if holding a memory of the sun

in the morning we swim to the diaphanous wings of dragons
tracing their ancient scripts on the surface of the water
where all grammars are dissolved

rasp of cicadas
lost celebrations of vesper bells
the melodiously long vowels of voices travelling
the length of the river

in the evening we sip tea from chipped ceramic mugs
our hands the woody joints of tropical bamboo
our silence the scent of apple blossom
and cherry blossom growing on the same branch

/

from an overhanging branch
the casting of petals on the river …
poems of many scents and various hues
beguile me

even those no longer here
relinquish their perfume as before

true to their scent
is realism enough

/

should we disagree
whether one is more
than the other

could we settle this
by counting?

would weighing tell us
what part of justice
is this love?

what part of the number
is odd?

begin again
and tell me that

/

when neither speaking or silence
can pass without error listen

to the short *waka* poem
as laconic and direct
as your answer

*

in my mid-sentence you lean
brush your lips against

that space the past alive
in our own flesh the words

unspoken once again you've
sealed them with a kiss

/

blossoms drop in ripening

one by one
tongue making

one by one
with swaying

hands on my hips
the artless accident
of the *sumi* brush

/

Sunday evening Bach on the clavecin
the angle of your cheek a cutting edge
the more love lasts the happy heart
forgoes its sigh the years pass by
plaster us over like beauty

(one wonders about the infinite numbers of possible
worlds God in order to be Best gives us an excess
of all that's best and all that's worst and God
being Good claims a surplus of good in this best
of all possible worlds so the worst could never be
held against Him this argument apparently good enough
for the Queen of Prussia)

/

the floor around my desk is littered with books crumpled
papers all the tools necessary to the engineering of poems
scales ruler a magic square an artesian well a compass
that keeps pivoting north a rhomboid…. the poem wants
precision the exact properties and relations of angles
and lines craves perfection the way a dog is perfected
by the huntsman's art

an oldie on a radio queries softly '… how deep is the ocean
how high is the sky …' inconceivable notions of depth and
height fables of landscape

it was for purely aesthetic reasons one philosopher wanted
the earth round and because the moon shines by reflected
light they came to the theory of eclipse someone must have
stood in a candle lit room covered one eye and moved a
marble back and forth between the other eye and the night
the outer ring of the moon visible around the marble
small ivory lunules on all sides the boundary between light
and dark never sharp

for Peter

your eyes are a million tiny organisms darting
in different directions each one carrying
its own aquarium a map I'll return to all my life

as a boy you loved sagas about Polynesians crossing
the Pacific without as much as a compass and Chinese
sailors building the first one to help them navigate
their seas

some claim a giant lodestone mountain
in the far north towards which they strain
while others feeling more maternal give magnets
a face a grin that fastens so they can never
get anywhere from here

*

vacant mouths gaping on the shelf sallow skull
of the eastern moon minus its black tongue bivalve
sunrise unhinged hollowed red tooth shell the closing
of their form postponed (it is because there are empty
spaces we are able to use them)

as a child I believed everything ever said would be heard
again the slow accretion of every word every sound
as in the conch my aunt kept against her living room door
when pressed to the ear the far-off roar of an island
a muffled heart a droning of no song

Let a better time say
The poet stopped singing to talk

Louis Zukofsky

1

It wasn't unusual in the early days
to rock the cradle of his son
with his left hand
while working on the electrodynamics
of moving bodies
with his right

in a cradle
the relative place of a body
is that part of the cradle
which the body fills and moves together
with the cradle

and relative rest
is the body in space
in which the cradle and all it contains
is moved
is rocked

one force
in its ellipse
about the heart
about the earth
around the sun

        light years bent by the rim
        caught by the cradle
        or the high sandstone ridge by the river Aare
        before their endless journey
        into time and space

        to the source
        nature's course
        light into body
        body into light

2

in his own time
in his own space falls free
from all magnetic fields
family friends houses

converts the universe
into perfect equations
fourth dimensions
of where and when

one man's now
another man's then

3

and there was his music
and there was his sailing
on the Zurichsee
or on Lake of Thun

the small red pennant on the mast
vertical for the sailor on deck
while it moved forward
for the bathers on shore

and for the gulls flying above
it fell back and disappeared

on the calm constant motion
of water there is no absolute

relativity is the only rule

4

formulas melted in his mouth
'give muscle to flesh' he said
'but to make them into bombs
would be like shooting at one bird
in the dark ...' and scribbled more
riddles on the back of old brown
envelopes where there is no bird

split the message
from the code
            alpha / beta

the flesh to bear the mark
of an equation the burn cold
metal gives as it unlocks
what's latent at the core
                    atomic

common denominator that spins
its own intrinsic chain of love
in quantities relative only
to the one who measures

5

On August 11, 1945
after Hiroshima and Nagasaki
Einstein is quoted in The Union-Times
'… we did not draw upon supernatural strength,
we merely imitated the sun's rays …
atomic power is no more unnatural
than when I sail my boat on Saranac Lake …'

by the

smallest

possible

margin

In spite of claims that his deconstructive method of analysis allies itself with the voiceless, the marginal and the repressed, Jacques Derrida doesn't much care for questions by women. During the seminars of his two week course, The Political Theology of Language, he spends at least fifteen minutes disseminating most questions from men, while he only spends two or three minutes disseminating questions from women and even then he manages to trivialize them to the point of eliciting laughs from the class. If in his texts, Derrida likes to question the masters, in his classes master and students stay in their respective places. In Derrida's seminars women remain seminally divided. Keep to the margins to bear witness to what he tells.

The course promises to focus on the discourse of 'the Chosen People', primarily the Jewish Nation, the differences and conflicts relating to their languages. It also promises to examine the values of promise, alliance, contract, mission, universal responsibility, messianism, and utopia. There are of course no women in utopia. In the kingdom of *différance* not all tongues are equal. The writers Derrida refers to among many others are Spinoza, Heidegger, Nietzsche, Lessing, Scholem, Buber, and when asked by one woman why women are so conspicuously absent from his material, he says that perhaps the best way to answer that question is to suppress it. This of course is the perfect answer and the woman never shows up again but another woman claims that he is the greatest mind of the 20th century so most of us hang on.

The first lectures deal with the signature of revenge. How history will seek vengeance on those who didn't understand the signs and whether vengeance is a human emotion or is it also worthy of the Divine? Since this is a course on the political theology of language God keeps creeping up, although as Derrida keeps reminding us,

God is nothing but a name, which is not really nothing but something. God is a sign. Perhaps that's why when we ask God to show us a sign, he never does because for God to show a sign would mean for him to show his face and if God is nothing but a name what could he possibly show us? You can't just think of God as mere subject acting as mediator, as interpreter. God as name is origin of the law and he can only maintain his role if he remains hidden, which means he can only be experienced as absence, as silence. He is what he is.

Considering that beyond the issue of language, the course deals implicitly with patterns of philosophical thought that may have led to the monstrous events that took place in Germany during the Second World War, the parallel that can be drawn between God as absence and the absence of women in Derrida's material seems trivial. It's not the right time to bring it up but like some spectral haunting neither will it go away. So I decide to say something.

It isn't easy to speak up in Derrida's class. He is after all, the greatest mind of the 20th century, which leaves very little room for exchange, but then Derrida doesn't seem that interested in the economy of exchange. He's more interested in the concept of the gift. Over the two week period he repeats at least three times how there can be no phenomenology of the gift, no awareness on the part of the giver that he's giving a gift. A gift can only be a gift if it's not a gift. He is delighted with his play of words and logic and we are delighted that he's delighted. As if we had all been given a gift. Except considering his definition of a gift I'm not so sure to what extent it is a gift or if I even want it. It smacks of a privileging of the present. A continuation of the past. The sacred power of a master's word.

I decide to speak. I am paralyzed. Aphasic. In view of God's absence, I propose a candidate, or at least an additional name for God. Derrida has pointed out via Schelling, that both religion and philosophy are lacking a mediator, an interpreter, or some semiotic sign and I propose to give him one by way of the amniotic. Thin membrane that surrounds all beginnings. The pregnant pause as conceptual space. Could the absence of God and the absence of woman, I ask, not be the same thing? Could woman only be a name? Absence?

His shrugging shoulders and emphatic 'yes' elicit another laugh. It suggests I have stated the obvious and to the greatest mind of the 20th century, I suppose I have. I should feel intimidated, but I don't. I don't feel at all as if I've lost face, on the contrary, it is inordinately conspicuous.

Oh I know what Derrida has written about the face. About the system that defines the face: its eyes, its mouth, its ears, which yield to sight, to speech, to hearing, but don't add up to a human being. How the I, in order to define itself, assert itself, has to deny so many elements of itself it can only differ from nothing by the smallest possible margin. The smallest possible sign. An apostrophe. Between nothing, between woman spoken, and a woman speaking in her name, there can only be the metaphor of the I, which like any other metaphor cancels. The sensory figure becomes imperceptible, obliterated, her presence suspended. She is nothing but a name.

But even an apostrophe in addressing absence turns that absence into presence. *'sophie*. Name of a woman, title of a book. On its own, a title has no meaning, which must be very uncomfortable for philosophers in search of meaning, but a title is at least a promise. Lives up to its promise by giving voice to words in which a figure is inscribed. Assumes a mouth, an eye, an ear, a face, the animated figure no longer separate from the fiction. No longer spoken she becomes at odds with what's been said. She is what she is.

Last night for the third time I watched Claude Lanzmann's film *Shoah. Shoah,* annihilation, a title, a promise. Nine and a half hours of interviews of Jewish eyewitness survivors, Nazi officers and functionaries, Polish peasants and townspeople who lived in the areas of the extermination camps. This is what's left from that moment of history. The verbalized memory of those who, for some reason or other, have been previously silenced, suppressed. Each 'I' the subject of knowledge that lies beyond the imagination. Each 'I', conveying the personal knowledge of acts which should be inaccessible to language. Yet, each gesture, each word pushed to the limit of its meaning transfers the unthinkable. Each gesture, each word, tentative, each person aware how words and pain always derive from the same source, always seem to lie in the other.

There is something else about the film that reaches so deeply, it compels viewing again and again. In contrast to the exhaustive interviews there are those long stretches of silence when the camera prowls the beauty of overgrown landscapes where there used to be extermination camps. The interminable train rides retracing journeys through cities and countryside emptied of voices and faces as if only silence could carry the weight of what's been said. As if only what has been said can carry the pain and beauty of a film when philosophy and God have grown silent in all languages.

espaces

vers

/

espaces vers vers où?
vers quoi?

cette rupture qui donne lieu à une syntaxe
qui se veut peau sur laquelle se trace un
autre sens (une sensation)

à travers le silence (les pulses travaillent en silence)
l'organisme se renseigne sur ses éléments extérieurs
(tes yeux ta voix tes mains) la mémoire d'un toucher
où s'inscrit l'au-delà d'une langue tout en insérant
de nouveaux fragments *oreilles neuves pour une musique*
nouvelle

/

/

tu m'avais déjà dit
que la langue arabe
n'a pas de verbe qui dit
je suis

c'est vrai
où étais-tu hier
pendant la nuit?

(c'est dans le vide que tout déclenche dans le noir les yeux
se conjuguent des schémas le cerveau se voit comme à l'écran
mise en scène d'un corps récit érotique l'amour concerne
toute la mémoire elle seule peut occuper ta place)

/

vingt-cinq ans

longue distance parcourue par un couple en mouvement
tous les deux s'emparant de l'espace et du temps
tous les deux à s'inscrire quoique tu demeures pour
moi absent

intervalle

petite dépression qui se façonne comme par un glacier
le nous du passé se dissout et pourtant la question
reste fondamentale qui a désavoué mon corps? qui
la métaphorisé?

le toi pensant au moi pensé?

d'où vient que l'amour et le philosophe
se représentent autrement?

presque j'ai perdu la langue au pays étranger
fille de langue pute fille de langue mal aimée
que jamais je n'arrivais à faire parler

c'est dans l'écoute d'une grammaire que le mot
devient pensée au carrefour de son corps où
se délit le son d'un coeur qui défaille entre
les phrases entre les idées pour retrouver
comme au premier jour son visage décomposé
afin de recomposer l'amant(e) l'aimé(e)

mi-dire *half thought half song when the passive voice of I am
spoken barely utters a kind of midspeak that speaks the part
the art of the half spoken that opens wide the middle ground*

demi-pensée demi-chanson intonation d'une voix
lorsqu'elle se réduit à l'essentiel s'en va au-delà d'elle
pour mieux s'entendre entre versions entre amours entre
philosophies

oser mi-dire (à toi qui ne fait que lire) comment expliquer
ce besoin? langue normalement organisatrice s'aventure hors
de son abri se trouve soudainement sans lieu tourne en rond
laisse échapper ses sons comme une bête son piège oraison du
désert sons-souches qui trainent les profondeurs de la pensée

je mi-dis donc je suis

à qui dire
je suis seule

j'ai voulu t'écrire
pour te donner corps
t'effleurer du mien

j'ai voulu fixer ma plume
au pied de ta lettre
aux points tendres de tes mots
mais ils se sont pensés autrement
comment te dire

t'écris-je avec trop d'amour?

qu'on te nomme idée
qu'on te dise cérébral
qu'on te veuille soupir de troubadour
phrases qui sont déjà

t'écris-je avec trop d'amour?

et si parfois je ne te résous pas
si cet amour ne donne plus lieu
qu'à une simple histoire
si je te décris pour mieux t'écrire

t'écris-je avec trop d'amour

et puis enfin l'amour
c'est ce qui se dit le moins

comment te dire?

si ce n'est que par amour

comment te dire
si ce n'est que sans amour

quel amour
nous sauvera

/

l'écrit creuse son centre
verbe clef du désir
creux berceur écoute à l'écart
l'espace qui se traduit à l'infini

d'avoir envie du rythme du pouls
de naître dans l'attente
de nommer au plus près l'innommable
de voir l'oeil qui décrit
d'entendre la bouche qui s'écrie
d'avoir la force de forger
d'avoir cherché jusqu'à ne plus trouver
d'avoir beaucoup exagéré
d'avoir perdu la peur de perdre
de m'être mise dans la tête
de m'être mise de tout coeur
d'avoir remis en question
d'avoir frapper le fond sonore
d'être arrivée jusqu'au moment
de m'être tenue à l'absence qui recouvre
d'avoir tapé sur le clavier comme au piano que je ne joue pas
de m'être tenue à une musique si peu articulée qu'elle forme
à peine une chanson

le chant du cygne se fait signe
laisse sa marque mais autrement
un livre qui se livre à toi

A Weekend at the Semiotics
of Eroticism Colloquium Held at
Victoria College

According to the brochure, the capacity to arouse and experience sexual desire has been a philosophical preoccupation since Plato, and the colloquium, 'The Semiotics of Eroticism', promises to examine new perspectives that have emerged through semiotic activity in recent theories and philosophy.

Considering that the great founding discourses of western philosophy, the *Phaedrus* and *The Symposium* are based on the amorous discourse, the erotic quest, which was far from being platonic and didn't have anything to do with women, I feel optimistic about the new perspectives. 'Beyond Eros', 'Fetish', 'Male Masochism and Subjectivity', … all topics that promise to examine current problems around eroticism and hopefully move beyond the explicit violence that Plato represents as the dynamics of the amorous soul.

The first speaker introduces his topic 'Darwinian Erotics: A Gene-Culture Perspective', and proposes to tell us why and how women have come to develop large 'garbanzos' or, if we prefer 'tits'. He beams at his own daring and goes on to examine the familiar darwinian theory of selection in primitive societies, something to do with male choice, childbearing and breast feeding.

The next speaker from The Medical Research Council in Scotland, illustrates charts upon charts of statistics relating to sex, desire and the brain and one of the conclusions drawn is that aggressive women, especially lesbians, have more male hormones than normal women. He doesn't mention if the same tests were performed on gay men, whether they have more female hormones than normal men, at least there doesn't seem to be any statistics on that and nobody asks. The next paper by a woman from Brazil deals with the Brazilian carnival and for almost an hour we are exposed to slides of women in scanty or barely existent costumes. The point being that during carnival time women are objects of the gaze, and the point is well taken since the man sitting beside me keeps making appreciative noises with each slide, while another man sitting across keeps rubbing his crotch trying to prevent a hard on. This is followed by a paper by a soft spoken man from India, 'The Erotic in the Classical Indian Tradition', which claims the equality of men and women in Indian myths and poetry. Then a paper by a psychologist concerned with the pathology of eroticism and the generally alienated sexual condition between men and women. Her argument is supported by astoundingly explicit slides of *Playboy* and *Penthouse* centerfolds as well as ads for various sexual aids, a vast assortment of devices that obviously required a great deal of imagination on the part of their inventors, including a cocky little number with the fanciful name of a thumper. Normally, the papers should be followed by a discussion period but no one seems to have much to add, except on the way out I overhear a woman say she wished she'd asked where she could get the thumper.

At home later on tv a famous sex therapist advocates the use of a small zucchini for women who happen to be minus a man. The host, feeling he's lost control of his show throws up both hands and walks off the set.

Hegel likened his to a thinking brain, the ascending and descending motions of. While Flaubert thought of his more as a tiger's tail with which to flagellate women. On that subject there's little point any more of going into what Freud thought.

A woman told me once how her personal vibrator had run out of juice, and she had frantically raided her children's toybox in the middle of the night looking for batteries, a ten inch GI Joe coming to the rescue. Doesn't care much for the average Joe anymore, for as Lois Lane says in the movie '… you're a hard act to follow Superman'.

song

of

songs

1

I was at your side then
remember?
your name and mine soft
unctuous fragrance our mouth drew

into your chamber
the upright love
philo kiss kiss

but now I am blue black
as a cloud before the sun
and our bed is never green

2

love's liturgy

Mozart on the tape deck winding
a voiceless *Lied*
song of the disowned

strummed over and over
a fear of no love that only love
can sire

where is my consort from the city of Marib
who always hung out by the moon of Almaqah
his hair a flock of sheep?

where will we fold at noon he and I
this other woman of frankincense
was I queen Sheba or Shulamite

holy whore from the wilderness?
myrrh between my breasts
blackroot of spikenard in my hair

it's been a thousand and one nights
since I went home to Moon Mother Bilqis
my lips a thin red thread

a thousand and one nights
wooing wisdom
speaking to myself

I am sick of love

3

had we been friends we could keep meeting
like this by the stairs keep whispering
in the voice of turtles (your hand on my thigh
a cunning)

had we been brother and sister
a seal upon our lips our words
would quench

had we been lovers
would I in your eyes …

but when you say love me
as thyself I can only answer
not yet not yet

4

a palm of carnelian
a cuff of fine silver
a mouth of far away

these were the gifts
of an anniversary

every marriage finds its image
in a song but if we can't
find the way to one another
young goats from the far east
will come to guide us

and should you not show up
by Friday the hahhuru bird
will nest in our bed
will avouch you dead
its words always self-fulfilling

5

I sleep
while my heart walks

your voice knocks
keeper of my walls

your hand in me I open
Shir-ha-Shirim

6

canticum canticorum
a little cant
a little cum
where only the wet phrase
holds an element of truth
mouth roofed by your soft
mouths off a richochet
of bilabial syllables
accelerates its triangular ligament
to let you ride
to let you ride my little
red little red riding hood

7

in everything that came to us unspoken held us at a distance
made us reach until the reaching paved the way towards
the assurance that we belong to everything that spoke to us
unspoken drew us into each instant that moved us into saying
each saying moving into everything that came to us unspoken
back and forth back and forth into saying

the connective tissue we hadn't counted on darkness
when the eyes give no sense of who we are or where
except for memory inside the palm that makes of touch
the test and brings back everything that came to us unspoken

8

the muse has learned to write

words fall gently in this weed and rain filled garden
their intimate touch awaken the measure of an extended
hand from which is offered another apple *un appel une pomme*
a poem the gold red rind of a rhyme *a rimmon* a garnet
the bony pulp of a pomegranate the acid taste of crimson the
sensuous pleasure of seeds that speak to the tip of the tongue
the curving stem of knotted rootstock the nodding flowers of
Solomon's seal it is all here in song in this weed and rain
filled garden (where voice is the site) its body distinct
from the metaphor so I can love you now that I am no longer
spoken for

Editor for the Press:
Christopher Dewdney
Author photo: Jerry Tostevin

For a list of other books
write for our catalogue
or call us at (416) 979-2217.

THE COACH HOUSE PRESS
401 (rear) Huron Street
Toronto, Canada M5S 2G5